INSTANT POT
COOKBOOK
for Beginners 2024

1800+ Super Easy and Healthy Instant Pot Recipes with Full-colour Pictures Easy Cooking with Time-saving Meals and Eat Healthier

Janice T. Jeffrey

*R*educe cooking time by more than half!

Deliciousness without the wait

Colorful pictures for intuitive cooking

DIY your recipes to your heart's content

Tips to be energized every day

1. Morning Exercise: Start with a quick workout.

2. Stay Hydrated: Drink water for alertness.

3. Balanced Nutrition: Eat protein, fats, and carbs.

4. Short Breaks: Stretch and breathe.

5. Positive Affirmations: Boost your mindset.

6. Power Naps: A quick recharge.

7. Sunlight Exposure: Mood and rhythm.

8. Deep Breathing: Stress reduction.

9. Socialize: Connect for energy.

10. Declutter: Organize for focus.

RECIPES

DATE

RECIPES		Salads	Meats	Soups
SERVES		Grains	Seafood	Snack
PREP TIME		Breads	Vegetables	Breakfast
COOK TIME		Appetizers	Desserts	Lunch
FROM THE KITCHEN OF		Main Dishes	Beverages	Dinners

INGREDIENTS

_____

_____

_____

_____

DIRECTIONS

_____

_____

_____

_____

_____

_____

_____

NOTES

SERVING ☆☆☆☆☆

DIFFICULTY ☆☆☆☆☆

OVERALL ☆☆☆☆☆

CONTENTS

INTRODUCTION 7

Breakfast 8

Appetizers, Soups & Sides 16

Vegan & Vegetarian...23

Beans, Rice, & Grains...30

Pork, Beef & Lamb 38

Poultry...46

Fish & Seafood..54

Desserts & Drinks 61

Appendix A : Measurement Conversions........................69

Appendix B : Recipes index 71

INTRODUCTION

Hello, I'm Janice T. Jeffrey, and it is my absolute pleasure to extend an invitation to you, my fellow culinary enthusiasts, into the delightful world of my Instant Pot Cookbook.

My culinary journey has spanned more than a decade, and my love for cooking has driven me to create this cookbook as a means of simplifying the kitchen experience for all. The purpose behind this endeavor is to make cooking accessible, enjoyable, and efficient. This cookbook is not just a collection of recipes; it's a culinary companion that will accompany you on a voyage of flavor and creativity.

Among its pages, you'll discover a wide array of mouthwatering recipes, some of which are brought to life with colorful illustrations designed to inspire your culinary imagination. However, I don't just want you to follow recipes blindly. That's why I've included Bonus DIY sections where you can tailor dishes to your unique taste, ensuring that your culinary creations are as individual as you are. For your convenience, there's a handy shopping list to streamline your grocery trips, estimated cooking times to help you plan your meals, and step-by-step instructions to make the cooking process smooth and stress-free. Drawing from my own experiences and challenges in the kitchen, I've also incorporated a treasure trove of practical tips, techniques, and insights to empower you and help you avoid common pitfalls.

Whether you're an accomplished chef seeking fresh inspiration or a kitchen novice eager to master the art of Instant Pot cooking, this cookbook is designed to be your trusty guide on a delectable journey of flavors and culinary discovery.

So, join me as we transform your kitchen into a canvas of culinary delight, and together, let's embark on the joyful adventure of home cooking. Happy cooking!

Breakfast

Ham And Swiss Muffin Frittatas 9

Savory Roast Beef Sandwiches 9

Sweet Potato Morning Hash 10

French Cheese & Spinach Quiche 10

Bacon Onion Cheddar Frittata...........................11

Georgia Peach French Toast Casserole.................11

Crustless Crab Quiche 12

Tofu Hash Brown Breakfast 12

Spinach & Feta Pie With Cherry Tomatoes..........13

Pecan Chocolate Chip Breakfast Oats...................13

Greek Yogurt With Honey & Walnuts...................14

Hard-"boiled" Eggs..14

Tomato Mozzarella Basil Egg Bites 15

Ricotta & Potato Breakfast 15

Breakfast

Ham And Swiss Muffin Frittatas

Servings:3
Cooking Time: 15 Minutes

Ingredients:
- 1 tablespoon olive oil
- ¼ cup small-diced ham
- ¼ cup diced red bell pepper, seeded
- 4 large eggs
- ½ teaspoon sea salt
- ½ teaspoon ground black pepper
- ¼ cup shredded Swiss cheese
- 1 cup water

Directions:
1. Press the Sauté button on Instant Pot. Heat olive oil. Add ham and bell pepper and stir-fry 3–5 minutes until peppers are tender. Transfer mixture to a small bowl to cool.
2. In a medium bowl, whisk together eggs, salt, pepper, and Swiss cheese. Stir in cooled ham mixture.
3. Place trivet into Instant Pot. Pour in water. Place steamer basket on trivet.
4. Distribute egg mixture evenly among 6 silicone muffin cups. Carefully place cups on steamer basket. Lock lid.
5. Press the Manual button and adjust time to 8 minutes. When timer beeps, quick-release pressure until float valve drops and then unlock lid.
6. Remove frittatas and serve warm.

Savory Roast Beef Sandwiches

Servings: 8
Cooking Time: 1 Hour 30 Minutes

Ingredients:
- 2 ½ lb beef roast
- 2 tbsp olive oil
- 1 onion, chopped
- 4 garlic cloves, minced
- ½ cup dry red wine
- 2 cups beef broth stock
- 16 slices Fontina cheese
- 8 split hoagie rolls
- Salt and pepper to taste

Directions:
1. Season the beef with salt and pepper. Warm oil on Sauté and brown the beef for 2 to 3 minutes per side; reserve. Add onion and garlic to the pot and cook for 3 minutes until translucent. Set aside. Add red wine to deglaze. Mix in beef broth and take back the beef. Seal the lid and cook on High Pressure for 50 minutes. Release the pressure naturally for 10 minutes. Preheat a broiler.
2. Transfer the beef to a cutting board and slice. Roll the meat and top with onion. Each sandwich should be topped with 2 Fontina cheese slices. Place the sandwiches under the broiler for 2-3 minutes until the cheese melts.

Sweet Potato Morning Hash

Servings:4
Cooking Time: 10 Minutes

Ingredients:
- 6 large eggs
- 1 tablespoon Italian seasoning
- ½ teaspoon sea salt
- ½ teaspoon ground black pepper
- ½ pound ground pork sausage
- 1 large sweet potato, peeled and cubed
- 1 small onion, peeled and diced
- 2 cloves garlic, minced
- 1 medium green bell pepper, seeded and diced
- 2 cups water

Directions:
1. In a medium bowl, whisk together eggs, Italian seasoning, salt, and pepper. Set aside.
2. Press the Sauté button on Instant Pot. Stir-fry sausage, sweet potato, onion, garlic, and bell pepper for 3–5 minutes until onions are translucent.
3. Transfer mixture to a 7-cup greased glass dish. Pour whisked eggs over the sausage mixture.
4. Place trivet in Instant Pot. Pour in water. Place dish with egg mixture onto trivet. Lock lid.
5. Press the Manual button and adjust time to 5 minutes. When timer beeps, quick-release pressure until float valve drops and then unlock lid. Remove dish from Instant Pot. Let sit at room temperature for 5–10 minutes to allow the eggs to set. Slice and serve.

French Cheese & Spinach Quiche

Servings: 5
Cooking Time: 20 Minutes

Ingredients:
- 1 lb spinach, chopped
- ½ cup mascarpone cheese
- ½ cup feta cheese, shredded
- 3 eggs, beaten
- ½ cup goat cheese
- 3 tbsp butter
- ½ cup milk
- 1 pack pie dough

Directions:
1. In a bowl, mix spinach, eggs, mascarpone, feta and goat cheeses. Dust a clean surface with flour and unfold the pie sheets onto it. Using a rolling pin, roll the dough to fit your Instant Pot. Repeat with the other sheets. Combine milk and butter in a skillet. Bring to a boil and melt the butter completely. Remove from the heat.
2. Grease a baking pan with oil. Place in 2 pie sheets and brush with milk mixture. Make the first layer of spinach mixture and cover with another two pie sheets. Again, brush with butter and milk mixture, and repeat until you have used all ingredients. Pour 1 cup water into your Instant Pot and insert a trivet. Lower the pan on the trivet. Seal the lid. Cook on High Pressure for 6 minutes. Do a quick release. Place parchment paper under the pie to use it as a lifting method to remove the pie. Serve cold.

Bacon Onion Cheddar Frittata

Servings:4
Cooking Time: 12 Minutes

Ingredients:
- 6 large eggs
- 2 teaspoons Italian seasoning
- ½ cup shredded Cheddar cheese
- ½ teaspoon salt
- ¼ teaspoon ground black pepper
- 1 tablespoon olive oil
- 4 slices bacon, diced
- 1 small yellow onion, peeled and diced
- 1 cup water

Directions:
1. In a medium bowl, whisk together eggs, Italian seasoning, cheese, salt, and pepper. Set aside.
2. Press the Sauté button on the Instant Pot and heat oil. Add bacon and onion and stir-fry 3–4 minutes until onions are translucent and bacon is almost crisp. Press the Cancel button.
3. Transfer cooked mixture to a greased 7-cup glass bowl and set aside to cool 5 minutes. Pour whisked egg mixture over the cooked mixture and stir to combine.
4. Add water to the Instant Pot and insert steam rack. Place glass bowl with egg mixture on steam rack. Lock lid.
5. Press the Manual or Pressure Cook button and adjust time to 8 minutes. When timer beeps, let pressure release naturally until float valve drops. Unlock lid.
6. Remove bowl from pot and let sit 10 minutes to allow eggs to set. Slice and serve warm.

Georgia Peach French Toast Casserole

Servings:4
Cooking Time: 20 Minutes

Ingredients:
- 4 cups cubed French bread, dried out overnight
- 2 cups diced, peeled ripe peaches
- 1 cup whole milk
- 3 large eggs
- 1 teaspoon vanilla extract
- ¼ cup granulated sugar
- ⅛ teaspoon salt
- 3 tablespoons unsalted butter, cut into 3 pats
- 1 cup water

Directions:
1. Grease a 7-cup glass baking dish. Add bread to dish in an even layer. Add peaches in an even layer over bread. Set aside.
2. In a medium bowl, whisk together milk, eggs, vanilla, sugar, and salt. Pour over bread; place butter pats on top.
3. Add water to the Instant Pot and insert steam rack. Place glass baking dish on top of steam rack. Lock lid.
4. Press the Manual or Pressure Cook button and adjust time to 20 minutes. When timer beeps, quick-release pressure until float valve drops. Unlock lid.
5. Remove bowl and transfer to a cooling rack until set, about 20 minutes. Serve.